Just the Opposite
Wet / Dry

Exactamente lo opuesto
Seco / Mojado

Sharon Gordon

Marshall Cavendish
Benchmark
New York

The park is wet.

❖

El parque está mojado.

The park is dry.

❖

El parque está seco.

The swing is wet.

❖

El columpio está mojado.

The swing is dry.

———————❖———————

El columpio está seco.

The slide is wet.

❖

El tobogán está mojado.

The slide is dry.

El tobogán está seco.

The bench is wet.

❖

El banco está mojado.

The bench is dry.

❖

El banco está seco.

The table is wet.

La mesa está mojada.

The table is dry.

❖

La mesa está seca.

The sandbox is wet.

El arenero está mojado.

The sandbox is dry.

El arenero está seco.

13

The sidewalk is wet.

La acera está mojada.

The sidewalk is dry.

❖

La acera está seca.

The playground is wet.

El patio está mojado.

The playground is dry.

❖

El patio está seco.

My class is wet.

❖

Los niños están mojados.

So am I!

❖

¡Y yo también!

Words We Know
Palabras que sabemos

bench
banco

class
niños

park
parque

playground
patio

sandbox
arenero

20

sidewalk
acera

slide
tobogán

swing
columpio

table
mesa

21

Index

Índice

About the Author
Datos biográficos de la autora

Sharon Gordon has written many books for young children. She has always worked as an editor. Sharon and her husband Bruce have three children, Douglas, Katie, and Laura, and one spoiled pooch, Samantha. They live in Midland Park, New Jersey.

❖

Sharon Gordon ha escrito muchos libros para niños. Siempre ha trabajado como editora. Sharon y su esposo Bruce tienen tres niños, Douglas, Katie y Laura, y una perra consentida, Samantha. Viven en Midland Park, Nueva Jersey.

23

With thanks to Nanci Vargus, Ed.D.
and Beth Walker Gambro, reading consultants

Marshall Cavendish Benchmark
99 White Plains Road
Tarrytown, New York 10591-9001
www.marshallcavendish.us

Library of Congress Cataloging-in-Publication Data

Gordon, Sharon.
[Wet/dry. Spanish & English]
Wet dry = Mojado seco / Sharon Gordon. — Bilingual ed.
p. cm. — (Bookworms. Just the opposite)
Includes index.
ISBN-13: 978-0-7614-2450-5 (bilingual ed.)
ISBN-10: 0-7614-2450-4 (bilingual ed.)
ISBN-13: 978-0-7614-2370-6 (Spanish ed.)
ISBN-10: 0-7614-1572-6 (English ed.)
1. Water—Juvenile literature. 2. Evaporation—Juvenile literature. 3. Polarity—Juvenile literature.
4. English language—Synonyms and antonyms—Juvenile literature. I. Title. II. Title: Mojado seco.
III. Series: Gordon, Sharon. Bookworms. Just the opposite (Spanish & English)

QC920.G6718 2007
551.57'7—dc22
2006017352

Spanish Translation and Text Composition by Victory Productions, Inc.
www.victoryprd.com

Photo Research by Anne Burns Images

Cover Photos by Jay Mallin
All of the photographs used in this book were taken by and used with the permission of Jay Mallin.

Series design by Becky Terhune

Printed in Malaysia
1 3 5 6 4 2

1|09 ② 1|08

4|10 ③ 3|09·

3|12 ⑨ 9|11

7|14 ⑪ 9|13

·4|18 ㉒ 12|17